W9-CNC-928

The
OBAMA FAMILY
Photo Album

Celebrating

THE INAUGURATION
OF BARACK OBAMA

in Pictures

Jane Katirgis

Enslow Publishers, Inc.
40 Industrial Road
Box 398
Berkeley Heights, NJ 07922
USA
http://www.enslow.com

For John

Library of Congress Cataloging-in-Publication Data:
Katirgis, Jane.
 Celebrating the inauguration of Barack Obama in pictures / Jane Katirgis.
    p. cm. — (The Obama family photo album)
 Includes bibliographical references and index.
 Summary: "Photographs illustrate the inauguration of President Barack Obama from the whistle stop train tour to the inaugural balls"—Provided by publisher.
 ISBN-13: 978-0-7660-3650-5
 ISBN-10: 0-7660-3650-2
 1. Obama, Barack—Inauguration, 2009—Pictorial works—Juvenile literature. I. Title.
 E908.3.K37 2009
 973.932092—dc22

                    2009009287

Printed in the United States of America

10 9 8 7 6 5 4 3 2 1

To Our Readers:
We have done our best to make sure all Internet Addresses in this book were active and appropriate when we went to press. However, the author and the publisher have no control over and assume no liability for the material available on those Internet sites or on other Web sites they may link to. Any comments or suggestions can be sent by e-mail to comments@enslow.com or to the address on the back cover.

♻ Enslow Publishers, Inc., is committed to printing our books on recycled paper. The paper in every book contains 10% to 30% post-consumer waste (PCW). The cover board on the outside of each book contains 100% PCW. Our goal is to do our part to help young people and the environment too!

Photo Credits: Associated Press, pp. 1, 4, 8 (inset), 10, 12, 13, 14, 16, 17, 19 (top), 20, 21, 22 (top and bottom), 24, 26–27, 30; April Saul; MCT/Landov, p. 6; Brian Kersey/UPI/Landov, p. 29 (top); Brian Snyder/Reuters/Landov, pp. 3, 19 (bottom); Dennis Brack/Bloomberg/Landov, p. 25; George Trian/UPI/Landov, pp. 8–9; Harry E. Walker/MCT/Landov, p. 18; Hou Jun/Xinhua/Landov, p. 29 (bottom); Jonathan Ernst/Reuters/Landov, p. 11; Kevin Dietsch/Bloomberg News/Landov, p. 7; Nikki Boertman/The Commercial Appeal/Landov, p. 15 (bottom); Ron Sachs/UPI/Landov, p. 28; Shannon Stapleton/Reuters/Landov, p. 15 (top); Suzanne Day/UPI/Landov, p. 31; Travis Heying/MCT/Landov, p. 23.

Cover Photo: Associated Press

Contents

Barack Obama Makes History

Crowds stand on a statue next to the National Mall in front of the U.S. Capitol. They are ready for the inauguration of Barack Obama.

*I*n the chilly morning hours of Tuesday, January 20, 2009, more than a million people gathered on the Mall in front of our nation's Capitol. They brought flags and blankets, signs and cameras. They came from near and far to witness a historic occasion. Barack Obama was about to become the first African-American president of the United States.

The inauguration was celebrated in a series of events, beginning with a train ride from Philadelphia to Washington, D.C., and ending with the last dance of the inaugural ball. The images in this book follow the American tradition of ushering in a new president. They also capture the excitement of the nation as Barack Obama became the 44th President of the United States.

Whistle Stop
Train Tour
Saturday, January 17, 2009

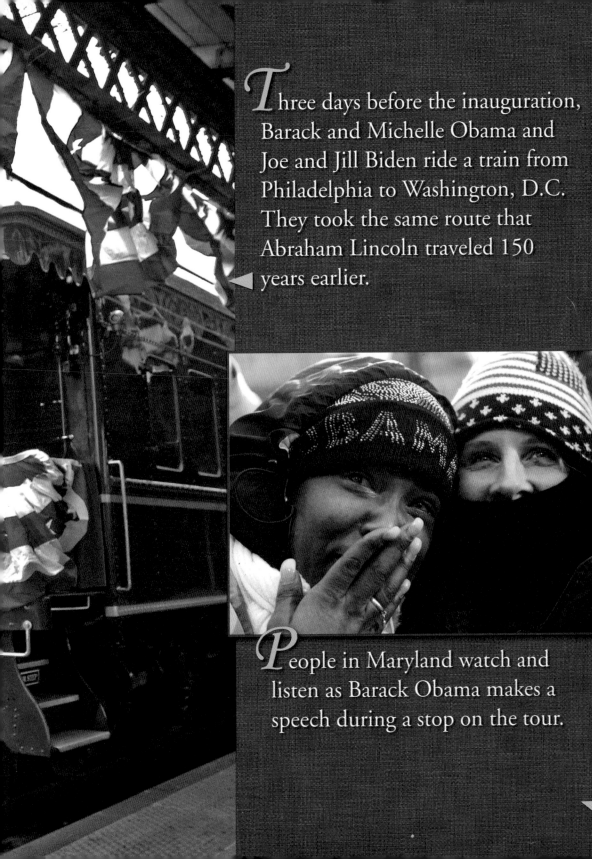

*T*hree days before the inauguration, Barack and Michelle Obama and Joe and Jill Biden ride a train from Philadelphia to Washington, D.C. They took the same route that Abraham Lincoln traveled 150 years earlier.

*P*eople in Maryland watch and listen as Barack Obama makes a speech during a stop on the tour.

"We Are One" Opening Inaugural Celebration

Sunday, January 18, 2009

*P*resident-elect Barack Obama speaks at the Lincoln Memorial.

Jill Biden, Vice President-elect Joe Biden, President-elect Barack Obama, and Michelle Obama wave to the crowd gathered at the Lincoln Memorial. The "We Are One" opening celebration included a concert and a speech.

National Day of Service

Monday, January 19, 2009

*P*resident-elect Barack Obama paints walls at the Sasha Bruce house as part of the National Day of Service Project in Washington, D.C. The house is a shelter for teens.

*M*ichelle Obama talks to a girl as she celebrates National Day of Service. She is helping volunteers make care packages for U.S. troops overseas.

Inauguration Day
Begins
Tuesday, January 20, 2009

*A*fter breakfast together, President George W. Bush and President-elect Barack Obama walk out of the White House. They are on their way to the Capitol for the swearing-in ceremony.

A Secret Service agent gets the new presidential limousine ready. It will take Bush and Obama to the inauguration ceremony.

Gathering on the Mall

More than a million people gather on the Mall for the inauguration of President Barack Obama. The Washington Monument is in the background.

15

Introducing
Barack Obama

$\mathcal{P}$resident-elect Barack Obama walks through an archway at the Capitol. He is on his way to the platform where he will be sworn in as the 44th President of the United States. He will be the first African American to lead the nation.

$\mathcal{M}$embers of the San Francisco Boys Chorus and the San Francisco Girls Chorus sing at the Capitol before the ceremony starts.

17

The Vice President Is Sworn In

As his wife looks on, Joe Biden takes the oath of office to become Vice President of the United States.

Music and Song

*A*retha Franklin, often called the "Queen of Soul," sings "My Country, 'Tis of Thee."

*M*usicians Itzhak Perlman (violin), Yo-Yo Ma (cello), and Anthony McGill (clarinet) perform an original song.

The Oath of Office

*B*arack Obama takes the oath of office. His wife, Michelle, holds President Lincoln's inaugural Bible. Daughters Sasha (far right) and Malia watch proudly.

*S*asha gives her dad a thumbs-up after her father is sworn in to office.

The World Celebrates

Students in Honolulu, Hawaii, enjoy an inauguration parade for President Barack Obama. They are at the Punahou School, where Obama attended grades five through twelve.

People around the world watch President Barack Obama's inauguration on television. The people are from *(left to right) top row:* Houston, Texas; Jakarta, Indonesia; Houston; *second row:* Park City, Utah; Denver, Colorado; Buffalo, New York; *third row:* Little Rock, Arkansas; Charlottesville, Virginia; Denver, Colorado.

Cheers erupt on the Mall as Barack Obama becomes president.

The Inaugural
Address

President Barack Obama gives his first speech as president. He is pictured at the center bottom of the photo.

President Obama waves to the crowd at the end of his inaugural speech.

Lunch with Congress

The new President has lunch with members of Congress. They eat in the National Statuary Hall in the Capitol. Notice the statues along the walls. They are sculptures of important Americans.

The Inaugural Parade

*P*resident Barack Obama and First Lady Michelle Obama walk along Pennsylvania Avenue in the inaugural parade.

*P*resident Obama and his family watch the parade from the viewing stand in front of the White House.

A band marches along the parade route on Pennsylvania Avenue, from the Capitol to the White House.

30

The Inaugural Balls

President Barack Obama and First Lady Michelle Obama get ready to dance at the Commander-in-Chief's Inaugural Ball at the National Building Museum in Washington, D.C. It is one of ten balls they attend that night.

President Obama and his wife enjoy their first dance of the night at the Neighborhood Inaugural Ball.

Further Reading

Books

Grimes, Nikki. *Barack Obama: Son of Promise, Child of Hope.* New York: Simon & Schuster Books for Young Readers, 2008.

Peterson, Christine. *The American Presidency.* Mankato, Minn.: Capstone Press, 2008.

Internet Addresses

Kids.gov. *The Official Kids' Portal for the U.S. Government.* http://www.kids.gov

The White House. *President Barack Obama's Inaugural Address.* http://www.whitehouse.gov/blog/inaugural-address

Index